WAS JESUS CHRIST A NEGRO?

- AND -

THE AFRICAN ORIGIN
of the
MYTHS & LEGENDS
of the
GARDEN OF EDEN

Two Rationalistic Reviews
By John J. G. Jackson

ISBN: 978-1-63923-137-9

Printed: November 2021

Cover Art By: Paul Amid

Published and Distributed By:
Lushena Books
607 Country Club Drive, Unit E
Bensenville, IL 60106
www.lushenabks.com

ISBN: 978-1-63923-137-9

Printed in the United States of America

WAS JESUS CHRIST A NEGRO?

- AND -

THE AFRICAN ORIGIN
of the
MYTHS & LEGENDS
of the
GARDEN OF EDEN

Two Rationalistic Reviews
By John J. G. Jackson

"That an imaginative and superstitious race of black men should have invented and founded, in the dim obscurity of past ages, a system of religious belief that still enthralls the minds and clouds the intellects of the leading representatives of modern theology – that still clings to the thoughts and tinges with it potential influence the literature and faith of the civilized and cultured nations of Europe and America, is indeed a strange illustration of the mad caprice of destiny, of the insignificant and apparently trivial causes that oft produce the most grave and momentous results." -- PETER ECKLER.

CONTENTS

WAS JESUS CHRIST A NEGRO?

A little over a half century ago Kersey Graves created quite a furor in orthodox religious circles by writing a book which flaunted the sensational title of *THE WORLD'S 16 CRUCIFIED SAVIORS* One of the most interesting parts of the book is a section in which the author discusses the racial identity of Jesus and offers evidence that the Christian Savior was a black man. The passage referred to reads as follows:

"There is as much evidence that the Christian Savior was a black man, or at least a dark man, as there is of his being the son of the Virgin Mary, or that he once lived and moved upon the earth. And that evidence is the testimony of his disciples, who had nearly as good an opportunity of knowing what his complexion was as the evangelists who omit to say anything about it.

"In pictures and portraits of Christ by the early Christians he is uniformly represented as being black. To make this more certain a red tinge is given to the lips; and only text in the Christian bible quoted by orthodox Christians as describing his complexion represents it as being black.

"Solomon's declaration, I am black, but comely, O ye daughters of Jerusalem' (Sol. 1,5) is often cited as referring to Christ. According to the bible itself, then Jesus Christ was a black man. Let us suppose that at some future time he makes his second advent to the earth, as some Christians anticipate he will do, and that he comes in the character of a sable messiah, how would he be received by our Negro hating Christians of sensitive olfactory nerves. Would they worship a Negro God?"

The question might arise in the mind of the reader: "Well, the argument of Kersey Graves sounds plausible enough, but really we need a great deal more corroborative evidence before we can give his conclusions more than passing notice?" This question, the writer believes, is justified. In questions of historical controversy only the most careful consideration of evidence should satisfy us.

To say that the early pictures and images of the Virgin Mary and the infant Jesus represent them with black complexions is not enough. Our statement must be backed up by archaeological evidence. This evidence, fortunately, was collected by the great British Orientalist, Sir Godfrey Higgins, and has been preserved for posterity in his monumental work; *THE ANACALYPSIS, OR AN INQUIRY INTO THE ORIGIN OF LANGUAGES, NATIONS, AND RELIGIONS.*

Sir Godfrey Higgins informs us that "In all the Romish (Catholic) countries of Europe, France, Italy, Germany, etc., the God Christ, as well as his mother, are described in their old pictures to be black, The infant God in the arms of his black mother, his eyes and drapery white, is himself perfectly black. If the reader doubt my word he may go to the Cathedral a Moulins - to the famous Chapel; of the Virgin at Loretto - to the Church of the Annunciata - the Church at St. Lazaro or the

Church of St. Stephen at Genoa - to St. Francisco at Pisa - to the Church at Brixen in Tyrol and to that at Padua - to the Church of St. Theodore at Munich - To a church and to the Cathedral at Augsburg, where a black virgin and child as large as life - to Rome and the Borghese chapel of maria maggiore - to the Pantheon - to a small chapel of St. Peters on the right hand side on entering, near the door; and in fact, the almost innumerable other churches in countries professing the Romish religion.

"There is scarcely an old church in Italy where some remains of the worship of the black virgin and black child are not to be met with. Very often the black figures have given way to white ones and in these cases the black ones, is being held sacred, were put into retired places in the churches, but were not destroyed, and are yet to be found there.

"When the circumstance has been named to the Romish priests they have endeavored to disguise the fact by pretending that the child has become black by the smoke of candles; but it was black where the smoke of a candle never came and, besides how come the candles not to blacken the white of the eyes, the teeth and the shirt and to redden the lips? Their real blackness is not to be questioned for a moment. A black virgin and child among the white Germans, Swiss, French, and Italians" *(THE ANACALYPSIS, VOL. I, BOOK IV, Chap. 1)*. My friend, Mr. J. A. Rogers, the well known traveller and journalist, has seen quite a large number of these black images of the Madonna and infant in his European travels and has discovered that some of the images possess African features. Evidently early Christians must have thought that Jesus Christ

15

was a member of the Ethiopian race or they would not have so stressed the dark hue of the skin of the Savior and his mother in their pictures and statues.

According to Christian dogma, Jesus is the son of God. Since children are, as a rule, similar in complexion to their parents it is reasonable to assume that God also is black. This conclusion is both logical and scientific. "There is a strong reason to think," declares Joseph McCabe, "that man was at first very dark of skin, woolly haired and flat nosed." And since the bible tells us that man was created in God's Image, then beyond all doubt God must be of dark complexion with unmistakably African features.

Some of my friend have suggested that should it be generally believed in these United States that either Jesus or Jehovah were of sable hue that the Christian church would soon go out of business. They reason that white citizens of the nation, on account of race prejudice, would have absolutely no use for a black God; and the colored citizens would not have any confidence in an Ethiopian God who had so long neglected his own race of people. However, I do not think such a situation will come to pass, for the overwhelming majority of people do not believe what is plausible of what is true; they believe what is comforting or pleasing.

THE AFRICAN ORIGIN OF THE MYTHS AND LEGENDS OF THE GARDEN OF EDEN

The Bible in its present form begins with a cosmogony. Cosmogony means a hypothesis or an account of the beginning of the world. *The Book of Genesis* contains two versions of the creation of our planet. The first, or Elohistic account, commences with the first verse of the first chapter of Genesis and ends with the third verse of the second chapter. The second, or Jehovistic version of creation, begins with the fourth verse of the second chapter of Genesis and extends through the twenty-fourth verse of the third chapter.

The reason these two creation stories are referred as Elohistic and Jehovistic is because of the different Hebrew names used in speaking of the Deity in the two documents or classes of documents from which our present accounts were derived. In the first story of creation the Hebrew word Elohim was originally used in referring to the Supreme Being. Elohim, translated literally *THE GODS*, is rendered God in our present bible. In the second story the original Hebrew word for god is Jehovah or Jehovah Elohim, literally the GOD of gods, rendered in the Kings James version of the bible as the Lord God. The differences between the Elohistic and Jehovistic accounts of the beginnings of the earth, plant and animal life and the human race theologian of the Anglican Church, Bishop John William Colenso:

"The following are the most noticeable points of differences between the two cosmogonies: (1) In the first the earth emerges from the waters, and is, therefore *SATURATED WITH MOISTURE*. In second, the whole face of the ground requires to be moistened. In the first, the birds and the beasts are created before man. In the second, man is created before the birds and the beasts. (3) In the first all fowls that fly are made out of the waters. In the second, the fowls of the air are made out of the ground.

"(4) In the first, man is created in the image of God. In the second, man is made of the dust of the ground and merely animated with the breath of life; and it is only after his eating the forbidden fruit that the Lord said, "Behold, the man has become as one of us, to know good and evil.

"(5) In the first, man is made lord of the WHOLE EARTH, in the second, he is merely placed in the garden of Eden, TO DRESS IT, AND TO KEEP IT.

"(6) In the first the man and the woman are CREATED TOGETHER as the closing and completing work of the whole creation; created also, as is evidently implied in the same kind of way, to be the complement of one another and, thus created, they are blessed together.

"In the second, the beasts and birds are created BETWEEN the man and the woman. First, the man is made of the dust of ground; he is placed by HIMSELF in the garden charge with a solemn command and threatened with a curse if he breaks it; THEN THE BEASTS AND BIRDS ARE MADE and the man gives names to them; lastly, after all this, the woman is made out of one of his ribs, but merely as a helpmate for the man.

"The fact is that the SECOND account of the creation, together with the story of the fall, is manifestly composed by a DIFFERENT WRITER altogether from him who wrote the FIRST.

"This is suggested at once by the circumstance that throughout the FIRST narrative the Creator is always spoken of by the name Elohim (God), whereas, throughout the second account, as well as the story of the fall, he is always called Jehovah Elohim (Lord God) except when the writer seems to abstain, for some reason, from placing the name Jehovah in the mouth of the serpent. This accounts naturally for the above contradictions. It would appear that, for some reason, the productions of two pens have been here united without any reference to their inconsistencies" (*THE PENTATEUCH AND BOOK OF JOSHUA CRITICALLY EXAMINED, VOLUME I, pages 171-173, London, 1863*).

Contrary to popular opinion, there is nothing original or unique about these Hebraic Eden myths. Similar myths and legends were told all over the world centuries before there was any sacred literature among the Hebrews. The Garden of Eden myth was anciently known in Ethiopia (Nubia), Phoenicia, Chaldea, Babylonia, Assyria, India, Persia, Etruria, China, Egypt and Mexico. The Hebrews first came in contact with these stories when the Israelites were conquered and enslaved by Sargon II, King of Assyria (722-705 B.C.). Thousands of Israelites were led into captivity by the Assyrian monarch. Colonists from the Assyrian Empire, which then included Media, Persia, Babylonia, Chaldea, Egypt and Syria, replaced the expatriated tribes of Israel. The ten tribes of Israel being overwhelmed and engulfed by their enemies were, as a result, absorbed into the polyglot Assyrian population, thereby losing their ethnic identity. This is how the famous lost tribes of Israel were lost.

Since there were originally twelve Hebrew tribes, ten of which composed the kingdom of Israel and two the kingdom of Judah, and since ten tribes of Israel were replaced by foreign colonists after the Assyrian conquest, it quite naturally followed that the two remaining Hebrew tribes of the kingdom of Judah were brought into close contact with these invaders. As a result these Hebrew tribes became acquainted with and adopted many of the myths and legends then current in the territories of the Assyrian Empire. They adopted not only the myths concerning the creation and fall of man from these nations, but also myths and legends of the Deluge, the Tower of Babel and others. There was a new and greater influx of foreign ideas after the Babylonian Captivity (586 B.C.).

Mr. George Smith, of the Dep't Oriental Antiquity British Museum, discovered Assyrian terra cotta tablets in Mesopotamia during the years 1873-1874, dating back as far from 1500 to 2000 B.C., which gives not only the story of the creation and fall of man, but narratives of the deluge and

Tower of Babel as well (See *THE CHALDEAN ACCOUNT OF GENESIS*, by George Smith, New York 1876).

A recent find of Dr. Chiera, Ass't Prof. of Assyriology at the University of Pennsylvania, throws new light on the Babylonian origin of certain legends of the Hebrews. Dr. Chiera's discovery is a tablet written in the Sumerian language. The inscriptions were carved on the clay tablet somewhere from 2100 to 2500 B.C. This tablet is thought to be merely a copy of a much older original, which in all probability dates back to around 4000 B.C.

In the original Babylonian Eden Myth there is the story of a great conflict among the gods. They cannot decide whether man ought to be created or not. A wise reptile, the age old dragon, Tiamat, opposed the creation of the human race. The dragon fought against the great god Bel. Finally the god overcame the dragon by hurling thunderbolts upon him. Opposition having been crushed man was created. This conflict between Bel and the dragon bears a close analogy to the story of the revolution in heaven recorded in the Apocalypse:

"And there was war in heaven: Michael and his angels fought against the dragon; and the dragon fought and his angels.

"And prevailed not; neither was their place found any more in heaven.

"And the great dragon was cast out, that old serpent, called the Devil, and Satan, which deceiveth the whole world;

21

he was cast out into the earth, and his angels were cast out with him" (Revelation, XII, 7-9).

This fable of a grand conflict between the forces of light and darkness in the celestial realms inspired the poet, Milton, to pen his immortal Paradise Lost. He pictures Satan as tall and handsome, majestic in appearance, brilliant in intellect. After recovering from his fall from paradise to the surface of a burning lake on earth he rallies his demons with eloquent and stirring oratory:

> *"Princes! Potentates! Warriors!*
> *The flower of heaven! Once yours now lost.*
> *If such astonishment as this can seize Eternal spirits:*
> *or have ye chosen this place After the toil of battle of repose*
> *Your wearied virtue, for the ease you find to slumber here,*
> *as in the values of heaven?*
> *Or in this abject posture have ye sworn*
> *To adore the conqueror? Who now beholds Cherub and*
> *Seraph rolling in the flood; With scatter'd arms and ensigns;*
> *till anon*
> *It is swift pursuers from heaven's gates discern*
> *The advantage, and descending tread us down*
> *Thus dropping; or with linked thunderbolts*
> *Transfix us to the bottom of this gulf.*
> *Awake! Arise! Or be forever fallen!"*

This warfare in the heavenly kingdom, with God and his angels on one side and the Devil and his imps on the other, was the central theme of the old Persian religion. Nowhere has the fact been presented with more brilliance and lucidity than in the following passage from Plutarch:

"Many suppose there to be two gods of opposite inclinations, one delighting in good the other in evil; the first of these is called particularly by the name God, the second by that of Genius or Demon. Zoroaster has denominated them Ormuzd and Ahriman and has said that of whatever falls under the cognizance of our senses, light is the best representation of the one, and darkness and ignorance of the other...

"The Persians also say that Ormuzd was born or formed out of the purest light; Ahriman, on the contrary, out of the thickest darkness; That Ormuzd made six gods as good as himself and Ahriman opposed to them six wicked ones; that Ormuzd afterwards multiplied himself threefold and removed to a distance as remote from the sun as the sun is remote from the earth; that he there formed stars and, among others, Sirius, which he placed in the heavens as a guard and sentinel."

He also made twenty-four other gods, which he enclosed in an egg: but Ahriman created an equal number on his part who broke the egg and from that moment good and evil were mixed in the universe. But Ahriman is one day to be conquered and the earth to be made equal and smooth that all men may live happy.

"Theopompus adds, from the books of the Magi, that one of these gods reigns in turn every 3000 years, during which the other is kept in subjection that they afterward contend with equal weapons during a similar portion of time, but that in the end the evil Genius will fall never to rise again. Then men will become happy and their bodies cast no shade.

"There is an apparent allegory through the whole of this passage," says Count Volney. "The egg is the fixed sphere-the world; the six gods of Ormuzd are the six (zodiacal) signs of summer, those of Ahriman the six signs of summer, those of Ahriman the six signs of winter. The 48 other gods are 48 constellations of the ancient celestial sphere, divided equally between Ahriman and Ormuzd. The office of Sirius (the Dog Star) as guard and sentinel tells us that the origin of these ideas was Egyptian; finally; the expression that the earth is to become EQUAL and SMOOTH and that the bodies of happy beings are to cast no SHADE proves that the Equator was considered as their true paradise" (*THE RUINS OF EMPIRES,* by Volney, page 139, Eckler Edition, New York, 1890).

The parallels between the Persian Eden Myths recorded in the sacred books of the Parsees, the Zend-Avesta and the Bundahish and those in Genesis are extremely striking. The Zend-Avesta account stated that Ormuzd created the universe and the first man and woman in six period of time and in the following succession: 1-THE HEAVENS. 2-THE WATERS. 3-THE EARTH. 4-TREES AND PLANTS. 5-ANIMALS. 6-MAN AND WOMAN. On the 7th day, Saturday, Ormuzd rested. The Avesta also records the name of the first man as Adama and the first woman as Evah.

Ahriman, the Persian devil, eats a certain fruit which gives him power to take on the likeness of a serpent. By persuading the first human couple to eat the fruit of a certain tree called Hom. he caused evil thoughts to enter their minds; this brought about their fall.

The Bundahish outlines the order of creation as follows: 1st period, Trees. 5th period, Animals. 6th period, Man-Woman. The reason for the hyphenated expression man-woman instead of man and woman is because, according to the Bundahish, the first human pair were a sort of Siamese twins. They were created joined back to back. They were divided later on by Ormuzd, who then admonished them to be humble of heart to observe the law; to pure in their thoughts, speech and actions. The man was called Mashya, the woman, Mash-ana and they were the progenitors of the entire human race.

Jewish tradition preserved in the *Talmud*, the *Targum* and, in the opinions of learned Rabbis, expressed the same point of view, namely that Adam was created at once man and woman with two faces, each fronting a direction opposite that faced by the other, and that the creator cut asunder the female half from the male half of Adam in order to give the woman a distinct personality. This idea of humanity beginning with such an hermaphroditic being is alluded to in Genesis as follows: "Male and female created He them; and blessed them; and named their name Adam in the day they were created" (*GENESIS, V.2.*).

The ancient Etruscan Creation Myth differs little from those of the Persians. The work of creation in the Etruscan legend covered 6000 years. In the 1st 1000 years, Heaven and earth were created; in the and, the firmament; in the 3rd, the seas and the other waters of the earth; in the 4th, the sun, moon, and stars; in the 5th, the animals of air, water and land; in the 6th, man (See Doane's *BIBLE MYTHS, p. 8, and Volney' NEW RESEARCHES ON ANCIENT HISTORY, pages 177-178*).

It is positively strange to find that these same myths and legends were current in ancient Mexico. The ancient Mexicans possessed a tradition of a war in heaven in which the rebellious angels were defeated. Also they declared the first man to have been made of clay and the first woman formed from a bone of the man. The Mexican Eve is represented on their monuments as the mother of two sons, who were twins; and again apparently in conversation with a huge serpent (See Maynard Shipley's *SEX AND THE GARDEN OF EDEN MYTH, page 46*).

The belief that the first man was made of clay was held all over the world in ancient times. In fact, the belief persists to this day among certain peoples. "The Ewe speaking people of Togo land in West Africa think that God still makes men of clay, "Sir J. G. Frazer informs us. "When a little of the water with which he moistens the clay remains over he pours it on the ground and out of that he makes the bad or disobedient people. When he wishes to make a good man he makes him out of good clay; but when he wishes to make a bad man he employs only bad clay for the purpose. In the beginning God fashioned a man and set him on the earth; after that he fashioned a woman. The two looked at each other and began to laugh." Sir James does not tell us for what reason, if any; "whereupon God sent them out into the world" (*FOLKLORE IN THE OLD TESTAMENT*, p. 11, New York, 1923).

A word ought to be said concerning the astronomical element in these legends for it is of greater importance than is generally supposed. Volney, building on the Solar Myth theory of Dupuis, found that the entire drama of the creation and fall of man could be traced among the constellations of the heavens. "In fact," declares that talented Orientalist, "take a celestial sphere painted after the manner of the ancients, divide it by the circle of the horizon into two halves; the upper one, the heaven of summer, light, heat, abundance, kingdom of Osiris, god of all good; the other half shall be the inferior heaven, INFURNUS, the heaven of winter, the seat of darkness, of privations, of suffering, the kingdom of Typhon, god of all evil.

"To the west and towards the autumnal Equinox the scene offers a constellation" (Bootes), "represented by a man holding sickle, laborer who, every evening, descends a lower and lower in the inferior heaven and seems to be expelled from the heaven of light. After him comes a woman, the constellation Virgo, holding a branch of fruit pleasant to the eyes and good for food. She also descends every evening and seems to push on the man and cause his fall. Under them is the great serpent, OPHIUCUS, a constellation characteristic of the mud of winter, the Python of the Greeks, the Ahriman of the Persians, whose epithet in Hebrew is Aroum. Not far from them is the ship, the constellation ARGO NAVIS, attributed at one time to ISIS, at another, to JASON, to NOAH, etc. And at one side is Perseus, a winged genius holding a flaming sword in his hand as if to threaten. Here are all of the characters in the drama of Adam, and Eve common to the Egyptians, Chaldeans and Persians; but which was modified according to times and circumstances.

"Among the Egyptians this woman, the Virgin of the Zodiac, was ISIS, mother of the little HORUS, that is the Sun of Winter which, weak and languished like a child, spends six months in the inferior sphere to reappear at the Vernal Equinox (the beginning of Spring), vanquisher of Typhon and his giants" (Volney's *NEW RESEARCHERS IN ANCIENT HISTORY*, pages 165-166, Boston, 1874. See also, the Plate: Astrological Heaven of the Ancients, in the Appendix to Volney's *RUINS OF EMPIRES*, New York, 1926).

There are a number of interpretations of the Eden Myth, the latest being a psycho-analytical explanation by Cavendish Moxon and a sociological hypothesis by Paul Lafargue. The solar myth theory has been mentioned in this brief survey because the author believes that the myth of Eden is, in the main, a solar myth. This opinion is strengthened by recent archaeological research. "The Babylonian Epic of Creation," states Prof. Stephen Langdon, the eminent English Assyriologist, "is based upon a solar myth and intimately connected with the triumph of the vernal sun and the spring Equinox" (*SEMITIC MYTHOLOGY*, p. 315, Boston, 1931). The fact that Volney recognized the true nature of the myth over a century ago shows him to have been a careful scholar of strong reasoning power and excellent judgement.

Though this little essay was meant to be descriptive rather than analytical it would not perhaps be advisable to omit altogether a consideration of the meaning of the several narratives of the creation of the world and the fall of man. As I see it, the myths of Creation are attempts of early man to explain the cosmos as it appeared to his untutored mind.

The myths of the FALL are based on man's yearning for immortality. Due to the habit of snakes of periodically shedding their skin, primitive man got the idea serpents were immortal. The natural vanity of man told our distant ancestors that the gods had intended the precious gift of eternal life for humanity alone. So the serpent was conceived of as having stolen this priceless possession from the human race and snakes have been very appropriately feared and hated by men from that day to this.

The biblical version of the Fall of Man is incomplete. The role of the serpent is not explained and the tree of life is not given due prominence in the story. The original story, which we are able to piece together from fragments gathered from the mythology of many lands in all probability reads as follows: God placed the first man and woman in a garden of delights. In this garden were two trees, the tree of life and the tree of death (called the tree of knowledge in the bible). Man had the choice of eating the fruit of the tree of life and becoming immortal or of eating the fruit of the tree of death and becoming mortal. God sent the serpent to tell Adam and Eve to eat some of the fruit from the tree of life so they might live forever, and to warn them against eating fruit from the tree of knowledge, or death, for if they eat this forbidden fruit they would surely die and this curse would descend to their children from generation to generation.

The wise and wicked serpent, however, reversed the message. He told the first human pair that they would gain immortality by eating fruit of the tree of death. Unfortunately, Adam and Eve believed the diabolical snake, ate the forbidden fruit and as a consequence were expelled from Eden and became mortal. The sly reptile, on the other hand, helped himself to the fruit of the tree of life and obtained immortal life for himself and his kind. God also punished the serpent for his disobedience by condemning him to crawl on his belly and eat dust. Eventually the second part of the penalty must have been revoked since it is a well known fact that serpents do not eat dust.

Though it is generally held by historians and scholars that the Hebrews got both their theories of the creation of the world and the fall of man from the Babylonians who received their civilization from a still earlier culture of the Mesopotamian valley, a people known as the Sumerians. According to ancient tradition, the Sumerians were originally a colony of Ethiopians. Though the Ethiopians were spread far and wide over the earth in ancient times their original home has generally been considered to have been located in the heart of Africa. In discussing the origin of the myth of the fall as recorded in the Old Testament, Sir James G. Frazer comments as follows:

"In favor of an African origin of the myth it may be observed that the explanation of the supposed immortality of serpents, which probably furnished the kernel of the story in its original form, has been preserved in several African versions, while it has been wholly lost in the Hebrew version; from which it is natural to infer that the African versions are older and nearer to the original than the corresponding but incomplete narrative in Genesis" (*THE WORSHIP OF NATURE, Vol. I page* 224).

Frazer infers an African origin of the Sumerians by stating that, "Even if the story should hereafter be found in a Sumerian version this would not absolutely exclude the hypothesis of its African origin, since the original home of the Sumerians is unknown" (*WORSHIP OF NATURE, Vol. I page* 223).

A good case for the African origin of early Babylonians is made out by Prof. George Rawlinson in the 3rd chapter of the first volume of his celebrated work, *ANCIENT MONARCHIES*. The following quotation gives the gist of Rawlinson's argument:

"The traditions with respect to Memnon serve closely to connect Egypt and Ethiopia with the country at the head of the Persian Gulf. Memnon, king of Ethiopia, is regarded by Herodotus and others as the founder of Susa. He leads an army of combined Susanians and Ethiopians to the assistance of Priam, his father's brother, and after greatly distinguished himself, perishes in one of the battles before Troy. At the same time he is claimed as one of their monarchs by the Ethiopians upon the Nile and identified by Egyptians with their king, Amunoph III, whose statue became known as the vocal Memnon.'

"Sometimes his expedition is supposed to have started from African Ethiopia and to have proceeded by way of Egypt to its destination. There were places called Memnonia supposed to have been built by him both in Egypt and at Susa; and there was a tribe called Memnones at Meroe. Memnon thus unites the eastern with the western Ethiopians and the less we regard him as an historical personage the more must we view him as personifying the ethnic identity of the two races.

"The traditions of the Armenians are in accordance with those of the Greeks. The 'Armenian Geography' applies the name of Cush or Ethiopia to the four great regions, MEDIA, PERSIA, SUSIANA, And ARIA, or to the whole territory between the Indus and the Tigris. Moses of Chorene, the great Armenian historian, identifies Belus, king of Babylon, with Nimrod. He adopts a genealogy for him only slightly different from that in our present copies of Genesis, making Nimrod the grandson of Cush and the son of Mizraim. He thus connects in the closest way Babylonia, Egypt and Ethiopia proper.

"To the traditions and traces here enumerated must be added the biblical tradition which is delivered to us very simply and plainly in that precious document, the *TOLDOTH BENI NOAH or BOOK OF THE GENERATIONS OF THE SONS OF NOAH.* The sons of Ham, we are told, were Cush, Mizraim, Phut and Canaan...and Cush begat Nimrod... and the beginning of his kingdom was Babel, and Erech, and Accad, and Calneh, in the land of Shinar.

"Here a primitive Babylonian kingdom is assigned to a people distinctly said to have been Cushite by blood and to have stood in close connection with Mizraim or the people of Egypt, Phut or those of Central Africa and Canaan, or those of Palestine. It is the simplest and best interpretation of this passage to understand it as asserting that the four races, Egyptians, Ethiopians, Libyans and Canaanites, were ethnically connected being all descended from Ham; and further, that the primitive people of Babylon were a subdivision of one of these races, namely, of the Cushites or Ethiopians and Libyans, but more closely with the people that dwelt upon the upper Nile" (*ANCIENT MONARCHIES, Vol. I, Chap. 3*).

Rawlinson's deductions were based, as we have just seen, on ancient tradition and history. An even stronger argument may be drawn from evidence furnished by comparative religion. All competent students of the origin and evolution of religions admit without hesitation that the gods of various peoples originally resembled very closely their worshippers, both physically and mentally.

Now, it is an indisputable fact that the great peoples of antiquity, both in the old and new worlds, were worshippers of BLACK GODS. For instance, Horus, the Egyptian Savior God, was black. So was Krishna, the celebrated Christ of India. So was Quetzalcoatl, Savior of the ancient Mexicans. Even Jesus, the Christian Savior, is represented in early Christian pictures and statues has having a black complexion. And all these black gods were the sons of BLACK VIRGIN MOTHER. Besides this, some of the great ancient nations frankly admit in their traditions that their religion came originally from Ethiopia (See Heeren's *AFRICAN RESEARCHES*).

In discussing the religion of ancient Mexicans, Maynard Shipley, President, Science League of America, asks two questions that certainly are food for thought: "How does it happen that the virgin mother of the Mexican Savior god so closely resembled the "Black Virgins" of Egypt and Europe? Had they not all a common origin?" (*SEX AND THE GARDEN OF EDEN MYTH*, pages 50-51).

Further on in the same essay he makes other comments equally thought provoking: "That ancient Pagan creeds, legends and myths, part of the universal mythos, should be found embodied in the religion of ancient Mexicans and all these again are found to be but original sources of modern orthodox Christian religion, is by no means inexplicable and need not be attributed to the subtlety of the ubiquitous devil. The explanation is that all religions and all languages of civilized races of men had a common origin in an older seat of civilization. Where that original center of culture was is another story. (*SEX AND THE GARDEN OF EDEN MYTH*, p. 60).

Gerald Massey, the English poet and Egyptologist, held this original culture center was in Africa. He brought up this question in connection with the subject we are discussing in one of his lectures published in London, 1887. In said lecture, "Hebrew and other Creations Fundamentally Explained," he asserted, "the legend of Eden is one of those primeval traditions that must have been common property of an undivided human race carried out into all lands as they dispersed in various directions from one center, which I hold to be African" (For an exhaustive defense of the theory of African origin of civilization and religion see first volume of Massey's work, "*A BOOK OF THE BEGINNINGS*").

Prof. G. Elliot Smith, the British anthropologist, gained no little fame in recent years by advocating the view that all civilization and religion originated in ancient Egypt. To paraphrase Prof. Smith, both civilization and religion are EGYPTIAN INVENTIONS. The school of anthropological thought represented by Elliot Smith and his disciples is know as the Diffusion School. In other words, they hold civilization originated in one particular locality and spread from there to the rest of the world. The opposing school of thought is known as the Evolutionary School. Their thesis is that civilization originated and evolved independently in many different parts of the globe. There is a third school, known as the Eclectics, who occupy a middle ground between extremes of the other two schools.

The science of comparative religion, as this review attempts to show, leads us to the conclusion that the diffusion school of anthropology has the best of the argument. However, since we have evidence that the civilization of Egypt is not the oldest in the world we do not abandon our diffusionist position by tracing civilization back to an earlier culture center.

My personal opinion is that these myths and legends of the Garden of Eden, besides many others of similar nature, had their origin in the heart of Africa in very ancient times and were spread by way of Egypt to the rest of the world.

Author's Note - Due to lack of space a few quotation were necessarily condensed.

www.ingramcontent.com/pod-product-compliance
Lightning Source LLC
Chambersburg PA
CBHW071807020426
42331CB00008B/2418